Learn How To Signal In Your Next Negotiation

How To Develop The Skill Of Effective Signaling In A Negotiation In Order To Get The Best Possible Outcome

"Practical, proven techniques that will help you get the best deal possible out of your next negotiation"

Dr. Jim Anderson

Published by:
Blue Elephant Consulting
Tampa, Florida

Copyright © 2013 by Dr. Jim Anderson

All rights reserved. No part of this book may be reproduced of transmitted in any form or by any means, electronic or mechanical, including photocopying, recording or by any information storage and retrieval system without written permission of the publisher, except for inclusion of brief quotations in a review.

Printed in the United States of America

Library of Congress Control Number: 2013923023

ISBN-13: 978-1494706166

ISBN-10: 1494706164

Warning – Disclaimer

The purpose of this book is to educate and entertain. This book does not promise or guarantee that anyone following the ideas, tips, suggestions, techniques or strategies will be successful. The author, publisher and distributor(s) shall have neither liability nor responsibility to anyone with respect to any loss or damage caused, or alleged to be caused, directly or indirectly by the information contained in this book.

Recent Books By The Author

Product Management

- Product Management Secrets: Techniques For Product Managers To Boost Product Sales And Increase Customer Satisfaction

- Customer Lessons For Product Managers: Techniques For Product Managers To Better Understand What Their Customers Really Want

Public Speaking

- How To Give A Great Presentation: Presentation techniques that will transform a speech into a memorable event

- How To Rehearse In Order To Give The Perfect Speech: How to effectively rehearse your next speech to that your message be remembered forever!

CIO Skills

- What CIOs Need To Know About Working With Partners: Techniques For CIOs To Use In Order To Be Able To Successfully Work With Partners

- How CIOs Can Make Innovation Happen: Tips And Techniques For CIOs To Use In Order To Make Innovation Happen In Their IT Department

IT Manager Skills

- How IT Managers Can Make Innovation Happen: Tips And Techniques For IT Managers To Use In Order To Make Innovation Happen In Their Teams

- Secrets Of Effective Leadership For IT Managers: Tips And Techniques That IT Managers Can Use In Order To Develop Leadership Skills

Negotiating

- Learn The Skill Of Exploring In A Negotiation: How To Develop The Skill Of Exploring What Is Possible In A Negotiation In Order To Reach The Best Possible Deal

- Learn How To Argue In Your Next Negotiation: How To Develop The Skill Of Effective Arguing In A Negotiation In Order To Get The Best Possible Outcome

Miscellaneous

- Power Distribution Unit (PDU) Secrets: What Everyone Who Works In A Data Center Needs To Know!

- Making The Jump: How To Land Your Dream Job When You Get Out Of College!

Note: See a complete list of books by Dr. Jim Anderson at the back of this book.

Acknowledgements

Any book like this one is the result of years of real-world work experience. In my over 25 years of working for 7 different firms, I have met countless fantastic people and I've been mentored by some truly exceptional ones. Although I've probably forgotten some of the people who made me the person that I am today, here is my attempt to finally give them the recognition that they so truly deserve:

- Thomas P. Anderson
- Art Puett
- Bobbi Marshall
- Bob Boggs

Dr. Jim Anderson

This book is dedicated to my wife Lori. None of this would have been possible without her love and support.

Thanks for the best 21 years of my life (so far)...!

Table Of Contents

TO GET WHAT YOU WANT, YOU HAVE TO KNOW HOW TO SIGNAL ..8

ABOUT THE AUTHOR 10

CHAPTER 1: TACTICS 101: GIVING AWAY NOTHING & BECOMING A LITTERBUG 15

CHAPTER 2: WHY PROFESSIONAL SALES NEGOTIATORS BUILD A HOUSE OF STRAW 19

CHAPTER 3: PROFESSIONAL SALES NEGOTIATORS KNOW HOW TO FLINCH LIKE AN ITALIAN 23

CHAPTER 4: ESCALATION POWER: HOW TO USE IT, HOW TO DEFEND AGAINST IT 27

CHAPTER 5: SALES NEGOTIATORS KNOW THAT THE PHONE IS NOT YOUR BEST FRIEND 31

CHAPTER 6: WHAT SALES NEGOTIATORS CAN LEARN FROM A FOOTBALL STRIKE (MAYBE) 35

CHAPTER 7: THE SECRET TO DEALING WITH DEADLINES: WHAT NEGOTIATORS NEED TO KNOW 39

CHAPTER 8: SALES NEGOTIATORS NEED TO KNOW HOW TO WAIT ..44

CHAPTER 9: WHY GOOD SALES NEGOTIATORS SAY THE SAME THING OVER AND OVER AGAIN 48

CHAPTER 10: 5 TIPS FOR MAKING PEOPLE SEE THINGS YOUR WAY..51

CHAPTER 11: HOW TO GET THE OTHER SIDE TO SEE THINGS YOUR WAY DURING A NEGOTIATION 55

CHAPTER 12: 3 WAYS THAT A SALES NEGOTIATOR CAN KEEP A NEGOTIATION MOVING FORWARD 59

To Get What You Want, You Have To Know How To Signal

The art of negotiation depends on your ability to successfully communicate with the other side of the table. An important part of this communication is your ability to signal to the other side what your intentions are. Likewise, they will be signaling to you what they want to accomplish.

This additional signaling communication channel provides a negotiator with a great deal of information and allows them to steer the negotiation in the direction that they want it to go. However, signaling is not easy to do and it can be difficult to learn how to do it well.

Signaling in a negotiation is not just one thing, rather it is a complete collection of different actions that you can take to send a message to the other side. These actions can include body language, escalations, and the use of deadlines.

Signaling is a subtle form of communication. It's not something that any of us are born with, rather we need to learn how to use this technique to express what we want to the other side. Our goal must always be to be using our signaling to show the other side how we can keep the negotiations moving towards an eventual deal that will be acceptable to everyone.

In order to become better signalers, we need to take the time to observe how signaling is used in other negotiations. What we'll quickly realize is that signaling involves the ability to patiently wait and the ability to repeat ourselves over and over again just to make sure that we're able to get our point across.

This book has been created to provide you with an understanding of both what signaling in a negotiation looks like as well as how you can develop the signaling skills that you will need. We'll examine how you can use signaling when making concessions and how to get the other side to see things your way.

For more information on what it takes to be a great negotiator, check out my blog, The Accidental Negotiator, at:

www.TheAccidentalNegotiator.com

Good luck!

- Dr. Jim Anderson

About The Author

I must confess that I never set out to be a negotiator. When I went to school, I studied Computer Science and thought that I'd get a nice job programming and that would be that. Well, at least part of that plan worked out!

My first job was working for Boeing on their F/A-18 fighter jet program. I spent my days programming fighter jet software in assembly language and I loved it. The U.S. government decided to save some money and went looking for other countries to sell this plane to. This put me into an unfamiliar role: I started to negotiate with foreign military officials and I ended up having to participate in the negotiations for large international deals.

Time moved on and so did I. I found myself working for Siemens, the big German telecommunications company. They were making phone switches and selling them to the seven U.S. phone companies. The problem was that the switches were too complicated. When it came time to negotiate a deal with the customer, the sales teams struggled to create an effective negotiating strategy. I was called in to bridge the world between the product functionality and the business impacts as they related to the negotiations.

I've spent over 25 years working as a negotiator for both big companies and startups. This has given me an opportunity to learn what it takes to both plan and execute negotiations of all sizes. When it comes to negotiations, I've pretty much been there, done that.

I now live in Tampa Florida where I spend my time managing my consulting business, Blue Elephant Consulting, teaching college courses at the University of South Florida, and traveling to work with companies like yours to share the knowledge that I have about how to prepare for and execute successful negotiations.

I'm always available to answer questions and I can be reached at:

Dr. Jim Anderson
Blue Elephant Consulting
Email: jim@BlueElephantConsulting.com
Facebook: http://goo.gl/1TVoK
Web: **www.BlueElephantConsulting.com**

**"Unforgettable communication skills that will
set your ideas free..."**

Create An Effective Negotiating Team At Your Company!

Dr. Jim Anderson is available to provide training and coaching on the topics that are the most important to people who have to negotiate: how can my team effectively prepare for and execute a successful negotiation that will get us what we both want and need?

Dr. Anderson believes that in order to both learn and remember what he says, audiences need to laugh. Each one of his speeches is full of fun and humor so that what he says "sticks" with everyone.

Dr. Anderson's Negotiating Training Includes:

1. How to plan for a negotiation: what information do you need and where can you find it?

2. What's the best way to explore how a deal can be created during a negotiation?

3. How can you bring a negotiation to a close without giving in to the other side?

Dr. Jim Anderson works with over 100 customers per year. To invite Dr. Anderson to work with you, contact him at:

Phone: 813-418-6970 or
Email: jim@BlueElephantConsulting.com

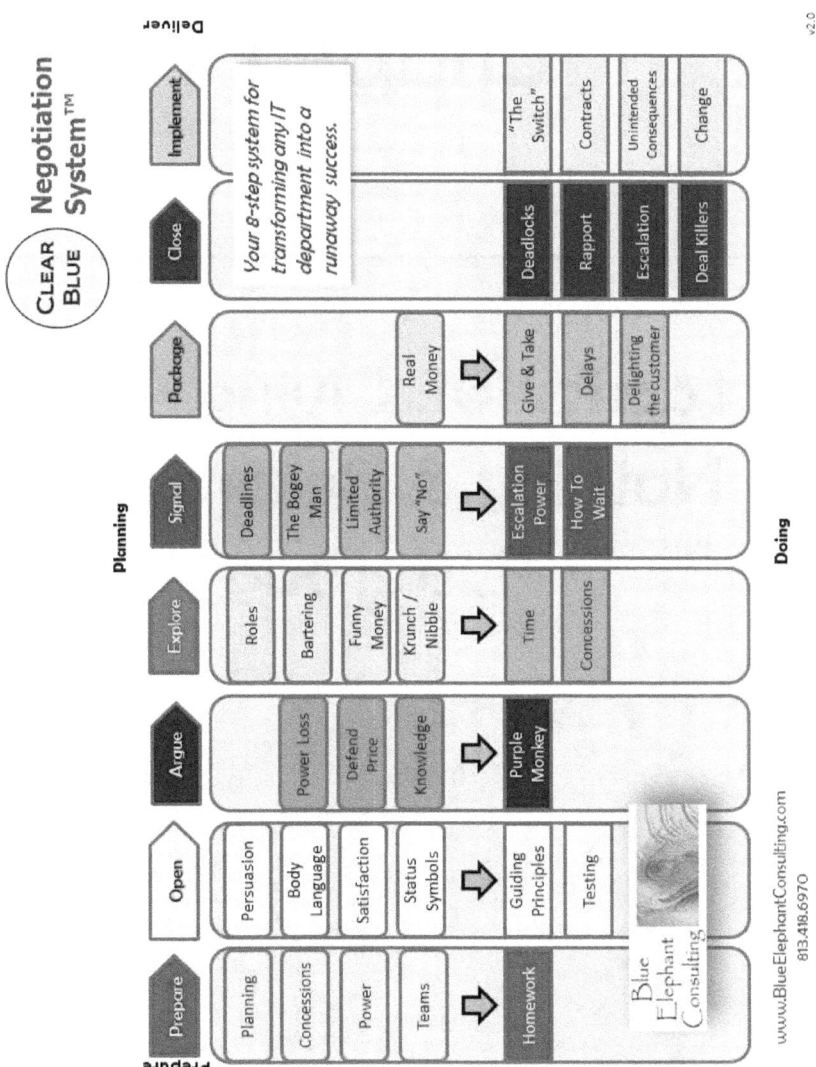

The **Clear Blue Negotiation System™** has been created to provide negotiators with a clear roadmap for how to manage a successful negotiation. This system shows negotiators what needs to be done and in what order to do it.

Chapter 1

Tactics 101: Giving Away Nothing & Becoming A Litterbug

Chapter 1: Tactics 101: Giving Away Nothing & Becoming A Litterbug

In the world of negotiating, the actual process of negotiating is very much an art. In order to be good at it, a master sales negotiator needs to have a complete collection of **negotiating tactics** at his or her disposal. Not every negotiation will call for every tactic to be used, but as any auto mechanic can tell you, having the right tool for the job can make your life a lot easier.

Empty Concessions Make The Perfect Gift

As a negotiator you will be expected to make concessions to the other side of the table during the negotiation in order to keep making progress towards an eventual deal. However, sometimes you may find yourself in a bind – for example, they want a lower price and you can't go any lower than you already are.

It is in cases like this that **empty concessions** can come in quite handy. Ultimately, the value of any given concession is determined by how the side that is getting it views it. This means that by identifying a negotiation point that means very little to you, but which means a great deal to the other side of the table, you will have found the perfect empty concession.

When you find yourself backed into a negotiating corner, an empty concession is exactly the kind of tool that you can use to increase the other side's **level of satisfaction** without having to give in on a point that is important to you.

Littering Really Isn't All That Bad

In some negotiations, it can seem as though the other side of the table holds all of the cards – you are at their mercy.

However, this is never the case. The concept of "littering on their lawn" simply means that you have the ability to make statements that will **cause them to pause** and realize that what you are offering them has more value than they had originally thought.

The following four examples show how negotiating litter can be made to work for you:

- **Value:** pointing out to the other side that yes, they could strike a deal with another company for a lower price; however, they would end up getting less value from the deal for the following reasons…

- **The Price Is Right:** sitting down with the other side and reviewing both your costs and your prices can quickly show them that you really are making a reasonable amount of money on this deal – not too much, not too little.

- **We're Different:** point out why comparing your offer to another firm's offer is not really an apples-to-apples comparison. Show that your firm actually provides many additional services.

- **Total Cost:** just focusing on the price of the item being bought or sold can be misleading. Taking the time to discuss all of the costs of the deal, both before and after the sale, can show that your total costs are lower than the competition.

What All Of This Means For You

Nobody is ever born a top-notch sales negotiator. Instead, we all improve a little bit during every negotiation that we are involved in. A key part of this improvement is making sure that **we know all of the tactics that we'll need**.

Concessions that mean very little to you, but which mean a great deal to the other side of the table are **a fantastic tool to use** when you find yourself backed into a corner. Casting doubt in the minds of the other side by littering on their carefully planned reasoning can cause the other side to become willing to reach a deal much quicker.

They say that knowledge is power and the more negotiating tactics you know, then **the more negotiating power you will have…**

Chapter 2

Why Professional Sales Negotiators Build A House Of Straw

Chapter 2: Why Professional Sales Negotiators Build A House Of Straw

In order to make your next sales negotiation a success, you are going to end up having to make some concessions. Knowing that you're going to end up having to do this means that you're going to need to have some strategies up your sleeve relating to how you want to manage your concessions. One time-honored way to make the whole concession thing work out for you is to use "**straw issues**". Let me explain myself...

What Is A Straw Issue?

A sales negotiation is simply a discussion about a set of issues. The number of issues that are being discussed can play a big role in the eventual outcome of the negotiations. The more issues that you have to discuss, the greater the probability that you'll be able to reach an agreement with the other side of the table.

This is where straw issues come in. Straw issues are throwaway issues that you put on the table. You really don't care that much about them; however, you present them to the other side along with your real issues. Their real value to you is in that they have an exchange value.

The beauty of straw issues is that the other side won't be able to tell the difference between your real issues and your straw issues. This means that they'll see your straw issues as being just as important as all of the other issues and assume that they need to be solved if a deal is to be reached.

How To Use Straw Issues

Face it – you're going to end up surrendering your straw issues during the course of a sales negotiation. This shouldn't be a big deal – that's why the straw issues are there in the first place.

What you need to understand is what giving up a straw issue is going to do for the negotiations. The other side will feel an immense sense of satisfaction when they "win" on the straw issue. It will be a trophy that the other side will be able to show to their management. Additionally, the negotiator on the other side will feel a sense of relief just because another issue is off of the table now – they are that much closer to reaching a deal.

How A Buyer Should Deal With Straw Issues

Straw issues are a buyer's best friend. You should make sure that at the start of the negotiations that you ask for more than you really want. This can include such things as the amount of time that you'll have to pay for what you are buying, increasing your credit limit, changes to the warrantee, etc.

Keep in mind that you won't actually get everything that you are asking for. That's not the purpose here. Just by giving in on some of the issues that you don't care about you'll make progress towards the negotiating goal that you want to achieve.

How A Seller Should Deal With Straw Issues

As a seller, you've got to realize that there will always be straw issues on the table during any negotiation. This can be a powerful internal tool for you: as you clear the straw issues off of the table your management will believe that you are doing good work.

Just because the other side of the table shows up with a lengthy set of issues that they want to discuss, don't despair. Recognize that many of the issues that they are presenting don't really count and work to find out which one's do matter. Most of the time you can get the other side to fold on most of the non-essential issues fairly quickly – unless they are an expert negotiator!

What All Of This Means For You

Half of the art of sales negotiating is knowing when to give in. It turns out that even this part of a negotiation can be managed. The use of straw issues can make your negotiating job a lot easier.

Straw issues are valid issues that you really don't care about. By including them in the negotiations you provide yourself with additional ammo when it comes time to make concessions. Giving in on a straw issue can make the other side happy while not eroding your position on more important issues.

In the end straw issues are one more negotiating tactic that you have available during your next sales negotiation. Study it and you'll understand how to use this powerful tool in order to strike better deals.

Chapter 3

Professional Sales Negotiators Know How To Flinch Like An Italian

Chapter 3: Professional Sales Negotiators Know How To Flinch Like An Italian

When you are involved in a sales negotiation, just exactly how should you behave? For some odd and unexplained reason, a lot of us think that we need to be stoic statues that never show any emotion.

Wait a minute. We're involved in a sales negotiation where we are trying to get the best deal for our side. We're not playing poker and trying to hide our reactions to our cards. Maybe it would be helpful to have a talk with some Italians to find out how we can become better negotiators…

The Italian Way Of Negotiating…

So first off, no, not everyone negotiates the same way no matter where they may come from. However, when it comes to negotiations, there are distinct styles that can be easily recognized when you encounter them. We can all learn important negotiating techniques from each style.

Simply put, the Italian style of negotiating is to be very expressive during the negotiation – the negotiator may or may not be expressing their true emotion; however, they are always broadcasting some type of emotion.

The part that is the most important to the rest of us is the simple fact that in the Italian style of negotiating you as the negotiator need to react to what the other side is saying in a visible way.

Why Your Reactions Are So Important

When you get right down to it, sales negotiations are simply a specialized form of business communications. Note that I said "communications". Although we tend to rely on our spoken words to communicate what we want the other side to understand, the reality is that we have a number of different ways to get our point across.

When you use the Italian style of negotiating, you involve your entire body in the negotiations. I'm not talking about going crazy here, but rather using your body to provide the other side with very clear feedback so that they can react in the way that you want them to.

The easiest and simplest example of this is when the other side presents you with a price. You might be tempted to look at the price and then put on your "poker face" and not let the other side know what you are thinking. But wait a minute, if you think that their price is too high and you think that you can get them to go lower, then you've got to let them know.

How you communicate your dissatisfaction with their price is where the Italian style of negotiating comes in. You've got a lot of options to choose from here. You can roll your eyes, you can throw your arms up, you can let out an exasperated sigh, etc. This probably is not a good time to get up and walk out, but that is always another option that you have.

What you are doing is using your body to provide the other side with clear and easy to understand feedback immediately. This will allow them to more quickly react and come back to the table with an updated offer.

What All Of This Means For You

Sales negotiating is all about establishing clear communications with the other side of the table. When we keep a stone face and display no emotions during a negotiation, we've cut off a critical communication path.

The Italian style of sales negotiations allows us to use our bodies to provide the other side of the table with clear, immediate feedback on how we think that the negotiations are going. Using our faces, hands, and entire body we can react to proposals made by the other side.

There is a note of caution that needs to shared here: you don't want to overdo it and come across like the actor Jim Carrey. Instead, use the Italian technique when you think that it will help you move closer to closing a deal. Just take the time to ask yourself, "How would Marco Polo react to that proposal?"...

Chapter 4

Escalation Power: How To Use It, How To Defend Against It

Chapter 4: Escalation Power: How To Use It, How To Defend Against It

When we're talking about negotiating and someone brings up **the tactic of escalation** what pops into your head right off the bat? Do you see yourself becoming frustrated with the person that you're negotiating with and getting up and storming off to go have a talk with their boss? That's one form of escalation, but that's not what we're going to talk about here – we're going to talk about the other type of escalation…

The Escalation Tactic

During a negotiation you may find yourself in a situation where you've taken your price down **as low as you can possibly go**. However, the other side may not have picked up on the fact that they've reached the bottom and they may be pressing for even more concessions from you.

Simply put, that's not going to happen. However, you need a way to signal to the other side that **they've gone too far**. At the same time you don't want to lose this deal. Clearly a clever tactic is needed here.

When you use the escalation tactic, you **revisit an issue** that the other side thought was resolved, you apologize, and then you change it. Most commonly this involves raising your price.

A case in point would be if you were close to closing a deal and all of a sudden the other side of the table started to make a series of demands for shorter delivery times or asking for more time to pay their bills. Clearly **you can't accept these kinds of demands** at this stage in the negotiations. By using the escalation tactic now you can go back and, after apologizing, raise the price that you had previously agreed to.

This is going to have **a dramatic impact** on the other side of the table. They're not going to know what to do – now everything is once again up in the air. Assuming that they still want a deal (and they almost always do), they're going to have to start to work to try to get the price back down to where it used to be.

By forcing them to do this, you will have effectively **moved the focus of the negotiation** from what they had been asking for back to the bottom line price. Once the original price has been reached again, the negotiations should be over and the issues that had been causing you problems should no longer be on the table.

How To Defend Against To Escalation Tactic

In the hands of a skilled sales negotiator, the escalation tactic is **a powerful tool**. That's why if you find yourself sitting on the other side of the table when the escalation tactic starts to be used, you're going to need to know what to do.

There is **no simple way** to deal with an escalation during a negotiation. What I can offer you is four steps that will provide you with a way to defend yourself against the full power of this tactic:

- **Call Them On It:** using this tactic resets the clock on the sales negotiation and is going to require that both sides invest more time and energy than they had originally intended to. The other side may end up not being willing to make this kind of investment. Challenge them and find out.

- **Pause:** stop the negotiations when the other side starts to use this tactic. This will give you time to consider both what they are now offering and will give you time to fully consider what all of your possible responses are.

- **Mirror Image:** hey, they are resetting the clock so why not do the same thing yourself. Review what's been agreed to so far and pick out one of their hard won points and state that you can't live with what's been agreed to and state that it's going to have to be renegotiated.

- **Hit The Big Red Button:** consider walking away from the deal. In fact, tell the other side of the table that you are considering walking away from the deal. See if this causes them to reconsider their use of this tactic.

What All Of This Means For You

Every negotiator needs to have **a set of tactics** that they can use in a variety of negotiating situations. Should you find yourself in a situation where the other side of the table is asking for too much from you, the escalation tactic provides you with an effective way to communicate to them that you are unwilling to budge.

The escalation tactic requires you to **revisit some negotiation point**, apologize to the other side of the table, and then undo the agreement that had been reached. More often than not this has to do with a previously agreed to price that you end up raising.

As a sales negotiator you are going to have to be careful when you use this powerful negotiating tactic. There are **effective counter measures** to it and if you aren't fully committed to what you are doing, you may find yourself putting the deal at risk. The escalation tactic is one more tool for you to have on hand so that you can use it when the time is right.

Chapter 5

Sales Negotiators Know That The Phone Is Not Your Best Friend

Chapter 5: Sales Negotiators Know That The Phone Is Not Your Best Friend

Isn't the telephone a wonderful invention? I mean just sitting there at your desk you can pick it up (or flip open your mobile) and reach out and touch just about anyone in the world.

It sure seems like **this must the best way to do sales negotiations in the future** – just imagine how much more you could get done! Hold on — the phrase "speed kills" comes to mind for a good reason – the phone may be the worst thing that has ever happened to sales negotiations…

It's All About Being Prepared

If you knew that you were going to be sitting down to conduct a sales negotiation tomorrow, **what would you be doing today?** I'm willing to bet that you'd be spending your time getting ready. You'd be doing all of the basic research, identifying what you wanted to get out of the negotiation, etc.

All too often this kind of careful preparation **seems to go out the window** when it comes time for us to pick up the phone and negotiate with the person on the other end of the line. For some reason, we don't seem to realize that we need to do at least as much preparation for this type of sales negotiation.

More often than not, our lack of preparation will come around and bit us in the end. We'll quickly **find ourselves backed into a corner** that we had not anticipated and in order to get out of that situation, we'll end up giving up too much and will wind up making a bad deal.

Speed Does Kill – A Deal

One of the reasons that things can go so badly during a phone based negotiation is simply **because everything moves so fast**. Before you know what's happening, you can find yourself in a very bad situation.

The beauty of conducting a sales negotiation over the phone is that **it can be a big time saver**. However, what seems to happen is that both sides of the table jump into the negotiation and start sharing way too much information. As human beings we can only take in so much new information at once and we quickly become overwhelmed.

Once this happens, **we start to miss important points**. This leads to us making mistakes. We'll also skip over key points that we wanted to bring into the discussions. As you can see, things will go from bad to worse.

But I Can't See You

In our rush to embrace new technology, it can be very easy to forget **why we do things the way that we do them today**. Sure, going to the effort of sitting down with someone and discussing a deal may seem old fashioned to many, but experienced sales negotiators will tell you that it's the best way to conduct a negotiation.

The reason that face-to-face is better than over-the-phone is simple: you can see the other party. Their body language, facial expressions, and overall demeanor **speaks volumes to negotiators who are willing to listen**.

The problem with negotiating over the phone is that **you are cut off from all of these other communication channels**. All that you have to go on are the words that the other side is speaking and the tone of their voice. These are good, but often they don't give you all of the information that you need to know.

What All Of This Means For You

Sales negotiators live and die by the deals that they are able to reach with the other side of the table. The telephone would seem to be a godsend – we no longer have to travel and meet face-to-face in order to negotiate. However, it turns out that **this efficiency comes with a steep price**.

When you negotiate using a phone it's all too easy to get involved in a sales negotiation **that you are not prepared for**. Additionally, things can move a lot faster when you are negotiating over the phone and you may find yourself getting lost quickly. Finally, when we negotiate over the phone we can't see the other side's body language. This is a huge disadvantage because what their voice is telling us may not be how they are really feeling.

We can't stop the future from arriving. More and more sales negotiations are going to be done over the phone and expensive face-to-face negotiations are going to be reserved only for the big-ticket items. This means that we need to remain very alert and **be aware of just how dangerous the phone is to our sales negotiations...!**

Chapter 6

What Sales Negotiators Can Learn From A Football Strike (Maybe)

Chapter 6: What Sales Negotiators Can Learn From A Football Strike (Maybe)

In the U.S. in 2011 there was the very real possibility that the national sport, American football, would not start its season on time because **all of the players would be out on strike**. What's amazing is that the National Football League (NFL) and the players were more successful than they'd ever been. The events that led us to this point provide opportunities for sales negotiators to watch and learn...

Football Has Been Very, Very Good To Many People

In the U.S., the sport of football is all about making (and spending) money. U.S. Football is **the most successful professional sports league in the world**. They are estimated to earn US$9B a year!

The NFL makes money in **three different ways**: they sell tickets so that fans can come and attend games, they sell broadcast fees to television networks so that they can show the games and sell advertising slots, and they sell corporate sponsorships to both individual teams as well as to the NFL itself.

Why A Football Strike Just Might Have Happened

If a strike happened, it could have gone on for months. When strikes like this have happened in other U.S. sports such as baseball, hockey, and basketball, **billions of dollars have been lost**.

The key point that could have led to a strike was simple enough: the owners and the players disagreed about **how to spend the**

US$9B in annual revenue that the sport of football generates. Right now, the owners get US$1B of that right off the top. The remaining US$8B is then split 60/40 between the players and the owners.

The disagreement came about because now the owners want to **take US$2B off the top** and continue to split the remaining US$7B 60/40 with the players. The owners say that they need these additional funds because their costs have been dramatically increasing. What this means is that the players would be taking a 12.5% decrease in pay.

Just to complicate matters, the owners want **two other changes**: they want to play an additional two games every season (more tickets, more broadcast fees) and cut pay for rookies.

The players say that they don't want a longer season because football is a rough sport and more games would mean that they'd have **a greater chance to get injured**. They are ok with the rookie pay cut, but they want the money saved to go to veteran players – not into the owner's pockets.

What A Football Strike Would Mean For Everyone

If a football strike happened, **there's going to be a lot of money lost**. First off, ticket revenue is going to vanish – if you don't play a game, then you're not going to be able to sell any tickets. Next, the corporate sponsorships are going to go away – if you're not playing games, then the companies are not getting their brands out in front of potential customers and so they are going to have to find other places to spend their money.

There was a good chance that a federal judge might require the football team owners to place at least part of their US$4B in television broadcast-rights fees **into an escrow account** until things got worked out. If they don't have access to this cash, at least some of the owners are going to be scrambling to find ways to pay the loans that they've taken out.

What All Of This Means For You

From a sales negotiator point-of-view, this very expensive possible strike should provide all of us with **a fantastic learning experience**. Both sides negotiated for over 10 days. They then agreed to extend negotiations by a week and the talks continued.

What you should be looking for during something like this is **what both sides say publically**. The press will be used to communicate bargaining positions to the other side. We should also watch to see what both sides actually do: are they preparing their members for a strike to happen, are they telling them that it's going to be a long strike?

Most of us won't be negotiating a US$9B deal anytime soon. However, all of **the standard rules of a sales negotiation** apply here: you need to prepare for the negotiation, power is a fluid thing that will change sides many times during a negotiation, and it's always better to show up with a good team that knows their roles.

Chapter 7

The Secret To Dealing With Deadlines: What Negotiators Need To Know

Chapter 7: The Secret To Dealing With Deadlines: What Negotiators Need To Know

Just how long do you think that your next sales negotiation is going to last? I've got news for you – it may not last as long as you may think that it's going to last. The reason is that either side of the table may use deadlines to help hurry things along. If this happens, will you recognize that it's happening and, more importantly, **will you know what to do when it happens to you?**

What's The Big Deal With Deadlines?

Are we all clear here on just exactly what a deadline is? A deadline is a device that can be used by either side in a negotiation **to move the discussion along**. Basically it's a way to get to the end of the discussions quicker.

Just because one side of the table presents the other side with a deadline **does not mean that anything is going to change**. Deadlines only work if the other side of the table believes that it's real. Oh, and sometimes they aren't – deadlines can be made up just to help the side that's making it up.

As a negotiator you've got **two skills that you need to develop**. The first is that you've got to be able to realize when a deadline is being used to motivate you to agree to a deal quicker. The other skill that you are going to need is the ability to deal with deadlines when they are presented to you. The good news is that both of these skills can be learned.

How Buyers Use Deadlines

Buyers are generally willing to work with someone who is trying to sell them something for as long as they think that they are going to be able to **get a good deal from them**. The quicker that they can get to a deal, the faster they can move on to the next deal. Deadlines are a powerful tool for buyers to use to accomplish this.

Buyers can use **a wide variety of methods** to impose deadlines on the other side of the table. One such method is to say that funding for a purchase will be going away quickly and so a deal must be struck soon.

Another is to say that they will be making a purchase, but if a deal can't be reached quickly then it will have to be made with another firm. Finally, stating that other parties will be involved in approving any deal and that they soon won't be available for some period of time is another time-tested method for buyers to impose deadlines.

How Sellers Use Deadlines

The other side of the deadline coin has sellers on it who like to impose deadlines almost as much as buyers do. Sellers are often working with multiple buyers at different firms and so they need to **determine if a deal is even possible** as quickly as possible. Using a deadline can help to get to the end of a negotiation quickly and this will free up time to work with other parties on other deals.

Sellers also have **a collection of classic deadline techniques** that they like to use. These include stating that a price increase is coming soon and the current price may not be available for much longer.

Tying the delivery date to the date that an agreement is struck is another way of establishing a deadline. Finally, stating that there is a limited supply of what is being negotiated for can provide the sense of urgency that comes with a deadline.

How You Can Defend Against Deadlines

Detecting that a deadline is being used against you is the first skill that you need to have as a sales negotiator. The next skill that you need to develop is **the ability to defend against a deadline**.

The first thing that you need to realize when you are presented with a deadline is that **it may not be real**. A deadline is just another negotiating tactic and you need to view it as being such. Do not allow a deadline to force you into rushing to make decisions that really require more time.

Instead, what you need to do is to **be skeptical about any deadline that is presented to you**. After having been presented with a deadline, your next step has to be to start to test it. Ask questions and dive deeper to find out what the implications of missing the deadline are and why they are tied to the deadline.

More often than not, you are going to discover that **a deadline is not a fixed thing**. Instead, a deadline just like everything else in a negotiation is up for debate and can be changed.

What All Of This Means For You

Deadlines are a powerful tool that can be used by either side in a negotiation. Instead of allowing the other side to believe that they have unlimited time to complete a negotiation, the use of a deadline causes the discussions to move more quickly with a sense of urgency.

Buyers use deadlines to move a deal forward so that they can either reach a deal with a seller or move on and start negotiations with another seller. Sellers use deadlines in an attempt to close a deal quicker. No matter who is using a deadline, when you are presented with one **you need to spend some time questioning if it is a real deadline**.

Deadlines will always be a part of modern negotiations. Your responsibility as a skilled negotiator is to be able to recognize when a deadline is being used and to then **know how best to deal with it**.

Chapter 8

Sales Negotiators Need To Know How To Wait

Chapter 8: Sales Negotiators Need To Know How To Wait

When we start a sales negotiation, we have certain expectations about **how it's going to go**. If we're selling something, then we believe that the other side will state what they are interested in buying, we'll have some discussions and we'll eventually provide them with a proposal. We then expect them to react to the proposal and that's when the real negotiating starts. However, what happens if they don't react at all…?

The "Hurry Up And Wait" Tactic

As negotiating tactics go, **the "hurry up and wait" tactic** is actually pretty simple. The basic idea is that the side of the table that is doing the buying takes over control of the pace of the negotiations. Once they do that, they are now in the driver's seat.

The selling side of the table has certain expectations in regards to what the next step in the negotiating process is and when that step will occur. When the seller takes control of the pace of the negotiations, **they can change the tempo** and this will cause distress for the seller.

A common way to employ the "hurry up and wait" tactic is to start the negotiations **with an air of immediacy**. Everything is rush, rush, rush. Discussions are held, requirements are gathered, and finally a proposal is made. Then nothing.

As the seller side of the table sits and waits for the next step in the process to occur (a response to their proposal), **they will start to grow more anxious** as nothing happens. The amount of time that is passing and the lack of feedback will serve to make them doubt that their proposal was a good proposal – especially if there are other sellers involved in the negotiations.

When the buyer side finally starts the negotiations up again, the seller side **will be so grateful** for any communications that they will be willing to make concessions in order to keep the negotiating process going.

This **start-stop-start process** can be used by the buyer side over and over again. As time stretches on, the seller side will become more and more disoriented and therefore more vulnerable to making poor concession decisions.

How To Counter The "Hurry Up And Wait Tactic"

The "hurry up and wait" tactic is a powerful negotiating tactic that puts much of the power during a negotiation into the hands of the buying side of the table. It is difficult to counter, but **there are steps that you can take**.

The most important step that you can take is to **realize what is going on**. Once you recognize that the "hurry up and wait" tactic is being used on you, you'll be better situated to respond to it. Your first step should be to notify the rest of your company about what is going on – this will remove much of the pressure that they would otherwise place on you to wrap the negotiations up quickly.

Your next step is to search for ways **to negate the use of the "hurry up and wait" tactic**. What you need to find is a motivation for the other side to move faster. If the item that is being negotiated is in limited supply or if there are potential delivery issues, you have the option of informing the other side of this. They are more than welcome to take as much time as they want; however, let them know that what they are negotiating for may not be available if they delay for too long!

What All Of This Means For You

During a sales negotiation, there are expectations as to **what the pace of the negotiation will be**. The buyer controls the pace to a great extent and if they decide to do so they can use the "hurry up and wait" tactic.

By alternating the pace of the negotiations from fast to slow to fast again, the buyer can **wear the seller out and induce anxiety**. This can cause the seller to start to doubt their price and therefore end up lowering it just to stay in the game.

Sellers need to keep their eyes open in order to **detect when this tactic is being used**. There is no clear-cut defense against it; however, being aware that it's being used is a good start. Sales negotiators who can detect when the "hurry up and wait" tactic is being used will be better prepared to roll with it and still end up getting a good deal.

Chapter 9

Why Good Sales Negotiators Say The Same Thing Over And Over Again

Chapter 9: Why Good Sales Negotiators Say The Same Thing Over And Over Again

I love to negotiate. Give me an objective, sit me down across the table from somebody who has what I want and let me at them. However, as gung-ho as I am, there are times that I **run out of new things to say**. I've said it all. What should I do next?

Say It Again Sam

When you enter into a sales negotiation, you (should) have a very clear set of objectives that you want to accomplish. Every negotiation is different and so it can **take a number of different paths**.

You'll generally have a chance to **state your case**. It's what happens after that which can make life interesting. Specifically, if the other side doesn't really respond – if they are not angrily attempting to counter your every demand, you may find yourself in an awkward situation.

The other side has not agreed to your requests, but they haven't not agreed to them either. **What's a negotiator to do?**

It turns out that the answer is rather simple – **just start repeating yourself**. That's right: say what you've already said once again. If when you're done, things are still getting quiet, then start it all over again and tell 'em what you've already told them.

Why Repeating Yourself Is So Effective

All of this might strike you as a bit wacky. I mean, if you've told the other side what you want and why you want it, what need could there possibly be for you **to start to repeat yourself?**

This might surprise you a bit, but there is a very good chance that the other side of the table **may not have heard what you said** the first time that you said it. There are all types of studies out there that show that people will do a better job of picking up on what you are saying if you repeat it (over and over again).

Professional speakers discovered this a long time ago and during their speeches they'll touch on the same points **multiple times**. As negotiators, we need to have the courage to do the same thing.

We need to realize that if the opportunity presents itself, then **we need to seize it**. Repeating ourselves may be the one thing that it takes to reach a deal in our next negotiation.

What All Of This Means For You

Even the best of us can **run out of things to say** during a sales negotiation before we've reached a deal with the other side. We've said what we had to say and now we're running on empty.

Never fear – a good sales negotiator knows that the sounds of silence need never drift across the negotiating table from your side. Instead, back things up and **identify your key points again**. Once you have them in hand, repeat what you said the first time – over and over again.

This odd but strangely powerful technique will allow you to fill the space in the negotiation and can **work miracles** – hearing your points again may cause the other side of the table to adopt them as their own. Realizing that not every word that tumbles out of your mouth has to be a novel thought is something that can empower every sales negotiator.

Chapter 10

5 Tips For Making People See Things Your Way

Chapter 10: 5 Tips For Making People See Things Your Way

The goal of any negotiation is to get the other side of the table to **see things your way**. Hmm, how are we going to make that happen? What you are going to have to do is to become skilled at finding ways to support the position that you are taking. In order to get better at doing this, I've got 5 tips that will boost your skills...

Tips For Reaching A Deal Faster

If you want to be able to reach a deal with the other side of the table faster, then you're going to have to take the time to give some thought to what it's going to take in order to get them to see things your way. In other words, **you've got some persuading to do**. Here's how to make that happen:

- **Move From Easy To Hard:** Experienced negotiators know that it's always a good idea to start a negotiation by tackling an issue that both sides are going to be able to easily reach an agreement on. Once you've got this success under your belt, then move on and start to tackle the tougher issues that are going to be more controversial.

- **Say It Again:** I know that I've said this several times before, but I don't think that I can say it enough – during a sales negotiation, it never hurts to repeat yourself. The more often that you say something, the better the chances that your message is going to be heard by the other side of the table and that it will be understood. Yeah, it might sound silly to you, but repeat yourself enough and you'll be amazed at what happens.

- **Understand To Build Trust:** One of the biggest challenges that every negotiator has is that they want to be understood by the other side of the table. What this means for you is that the more that the other side believes that you understand what they are saying (and why they are saying it), the better your chances of reaching a deal are. Take the time to show the other side that you get what they are saying and you'll build trust with them which will lead to greater cooperation.

- **Head Off Issues Early:** As part of your planning for your next negotiation, you need to take a look at all of the issues that will be discussed. Not all issues are created the same. For those issues that you know that are going to create resistance from the other side of the table, you need to be proactive and take action before they are even brought up. What you are going to want to do is to defuse the issue so that when both sides start to discuss it in earnest, it's no longer such a controversial issue.

- **Success By Association:** If there is an issue that will be part of your next negotiation that has a great deal of controversy associated with it and there is no way to defuse it, then you've got to get creative. If the issue gets discussed by itself, you're going to be in for a rough time. However, if you can find a way to associate this controversial issue with another issue that is less controversial then you'll be more likely to be able to reach agreement on it.

What All Of This Means For You

Every negotiation has the same goal in mind: finding a way for all parties involved to **reach a successful deal**. The challenge comes from finding a way to get from where everyone starts out to agreeing on that deal in the end.

Skilled negotiators know that they need find ways to **support their position** if they want to have any hope of reaching a deal in a reasonable amount of time. In order to make this happen, you can use the 5 tips that we've discussed in order to steer the other side of the table towards the deal that you want to strike. Try them out and you'll be amazed at how much quicker you're able to wrap-up your next negotiating session!

Chapter 11

How To Get The Other Side To See Things Your Way During A Negotiation

Chapter 11: How To Get The Other Side To See Things Your Way During A Negotiation

Every time you enter into a negotiation, you have one objective: you want to find a way to reach a deal with the other side of the table. Ultimately, if this is going to happen, then you are going to have to find a way to get the other side to **see things your way**. You know how you see the world, now how can you get them to see it the same way? I've got 5 tips that will boost your ability to make this happen...

Tips For Reaching A Deal Faster

In order to be able to reach a deal with the other side of the table faster, then you're going to have to give some thought to understanding how to get them to see things your way. This means that **you've got some persuading to do**. Here's how you can make that happen:

- **Do You Want Me?:** It turns out that all of us, including the other side of the table really want to be courted. We want others to want us and to take action to win our favor. The other side of the table will be looking for you to complement them, to say nice things to them, to be friendly towards them, and to listen closely to what they have to say. Doing this will win them over to your side.

- **Numbers Don't Lie:** There is something almost magical about facts & figures. When one side of the negotiating table presents a set of numbers both sides seem to accept them as being set in stone – they are numbers so they have to be correct, right? You need to be aware that all numbers always need to be challenged when the other side introduces them; however, feel free to bring your own numbers to the negotiating table and watch the other side start to see things your way.

- **More Is Better:** A very peculiar characteristic of us humans is that if one side of the negotiating table asks for something that is going to require a large change of opinion on our part, then they are more likely to get it than if they ask for a smaller change of opinion. The reasons for this are a bit mysterious, but it seems to have something to do with the fact that we can get our hands around small requests and this means that we'll debate them more. Bigger requests seem to go through with less discussion. Always request more.

- **I Recognize This Request:** Your ability to get the other side of the table to see things your way will be improved if you take the time to shape your requests. The more that you make your request "look" like something that the other side has already agreed to, then the better your chances are of reaching agreement with them. Acceptance is increased the fewer differences there are.

- **Show Your Cards:** Novice negotiators sometimes think that they can get away with pulling a fast one by just presenting one side of an issue. It's their hope that if they talk quickly enough and use enough words, the other side will somehow forget that there is another side to the issue. This never happens. What does happen is that the other side realizes that you are trying to fool them and any spirit of cooperation that may have existed in the negotiation is now gone.

What All Of This Means For You

Every negotiation has the same goal in mind: finding a way for all parties involved to **reach a successful deal**. The challenge comes from finding a way to get from where everyone starts out to agreeing on that deal in the end.

Skilled negotiators know that they need find ways to **support their position** if they want to have any hope of reaching a deal in a reasonable amount of time. In order to make this happen, you can use the 5 tips that we've discussed in order to steer the other side of the table towards the deal that you want to strike. Try them out and you'll be amazed at how much quicker you're able to wrap-up your next negotiating session!

Chapter 12

3 Ways That A Sales Negotiator Can Keep A Negotiation Moving Forward

Chapter 12: 3 Ways That A Sales Negotiator Can Keep A Negotiation Moving Forward

In every negotiation, you'll eventually **run out of things to say to the other side of the table**. I mean, come on, you've already said everything. In fact you may have already said everything more than once! You need to be careful when this happens; either side may feel like giving up without having reached an agreement. Never fear, I've got 3 techniques that you can use when you encounter this situation that are guaranteed to turn things around:

Use The Power Of "Win-Win"

We all know about the famous "win-win" negotiating technique. However, what you may not know is that **just by mentioning this technique** you can breathe new life into a negotiation that has run out of steam.

We all respond positively when someone suggests that we **"find a way to make this work out for both of us"**. The other side will perk up when they hear you say this and a negotiation that looked like it was over will have found its second wind.

Find The Path Of Least Resistance

I can't tell you how many times I've been involved in a negotiation and we've run into an issue that just **brings everything to a halt**. It sure looks like there is not going to be a way to resolve this issue and that means that the whole negotiation is in jeopardy.

It turns out that things don't have to end this way. Instead, you can seek the path of least resistance. Pick another issue that needs to be discussed and **move the discussion to this issue**.

What I find happens is you'll be able to reach an agreement on a number of these smaller issues and then when you finally come back to the "big" issue, it won't seem so large the second time around. You'll be able to resolve it and a deal will finally be reached.

Say "Yes" One More Time

Experienced negotiators know that **the simple word "yes"** has the power to move a stalled negotiation forward. What this means is that you always want to have another "yes" in your pocket ready to use.

This means that you need to be **aware of all of the issues that are being negotiated**. There are always some issues that you'll have no problem agreeing to with the other side. You need to keep a few of these issues off of the negotiating table early on in the discussions.

If things bog down and progress stops, then you'll know what to do. Bring one of these issues up, say "yes" to them, and watch the negotiations **get started once again**.

What All Of This Means For You

Every sales negotiation has its own set of **highs and lows**. There will be times in which you are in synch with the other side of the table and you are able to rapidly make progress on a large number of issues.

However, there will also be times when the negotiations start to drag. When this happens it may seem as though there is no way to move forward. Experienced sales negotiators know that it's always possible to make progress – you just need to know **what to do** to get things started again.

We've discussed **three techniques** that you can use: win-win, the path of least resistance, and saying "yes". Every negotiating situation is different and you'll need to make the decision as to which technique is going to work the best for you.

It's from the forge of failure that the steel of success is formed.

Hard Work Does Not Guarantee Success, But Success Does Not Happen Without Hard Work.

- Dr. Jim Anderson

Create An Effective Negotiating Team At Your Company!

Dr. Jim Anderson is available to provide training and coaching on the topics that are the most important to people who have to negotiate: how can my team effectively prepare for and execute a successful negotiation that will get us what we both want and need?

Dr. Anderson believes that in order to both learn and remember what he says, audiences need to laugh. Each one of his speeches is full of fun and humor so that what he says "sticks" with everyone.

Dr. Anderson's Negotiating Training Includes:

1. How to plan for a negotiation: what information do you need and where can you find it?

2. What's the best way to explore how a deal can be created during a negotiation?

3. How can you bring a negotiation to a close without giving in to the other side?

Dr. Jim Anderson works with over 100 customers per year. To invite Dr. Anderson to work with you, contact him at:

Phone: 813-418-6970 or
Email: jim@BlueElephantConsulting.com

Photo Credits:

Cover - By: grendelkhan
http://www.flickr.com/photos/grendelkhan/

Chapter 1 - By: Rik Panganiban
http://www.flickr.com/photos/rikomatic/

Chapter 2 - By: John and Melanie (Illingworth) Kotsopoulos
http://www.flickr.com/photos/melanieandjohn/

Chapter 3 - By: Ed Yourdon
http://www.flickr.com/photos/yourdon/

Chapter 4 - By: David Wise
http://www.flickr.com/photos/syldavia/

Chapter 5 - By: Valerio Graziani
http://www.flickr.com/photos/9436060@N06/

Chapter 6 - By: Ed Yourdon
http://www.flickr.com/photos/yourdon/

Chapter 7 - By: openDemocracy
http://www.flickr.com/photos/opendemocracy/

Chapter 8 - By: kobiz7
http://www.flickr.com/photos/27369469@N08/

Chapter 9 - By: Cindy Cornett Seigle
http://www.flickr.com/photos/cindy47452/

Chapter 10 - By: Ben Andreas Harding
http://www.flickr.com/photos/38605609@N02/

Chapter 11 - By: Len Matthews
http://www.flickr.com/photos/mythoto/

Chapter 12 - By: alan berning
http://www.flickr.com/photos/14617207@N00/

Other Books By The Author

Product Management

- Product Management Secrets: Techniques For Product Managers To Boost Product Sales And Increase Customer Satisfaction

- Product Development Lessons For Product Managers: How Product Managers Can Create Successful Products

- Customer Lessons For Product Managers: Techniques For Product Managers To Better Understand What Their Customers Really Want

- Product Failure Lessons For Product Managers: Examples Of Products That Have Failed For Product Managers To Learn From

- Communication Skills For Product Managers: The Communication Skills That Product Managers Need To Know How To Use In Order To Have A Successful Product

- How To Have A Successful Product Manager Career: The Things That You Need To Be Doing TODAY In Order To Have A Successful Product Manager Career

- Product Manager Product Success: How to keep your product on track and make it become a success

Public Speaking

- How To Give A Great Presentation: Presentation techniques that will transform a speech into a memorable event

- How To Rehearse In Order To Give The Perfect Speech: How to effectively rehearse your next speech to that your message be remembered forever!

- Secrets To Creating The Perfect Speech: How to create a speech that will make your message be remembered forever!

- Secrets To Organizing The Perfect Speech: How to organize the best speech of your life!

- Secrets To Planning The Perfect Speech: How to plan to give the best speech of your life

- How To Show What You Mean During A Presentation: How to use visual techniques to transform a speech into a memorable event

CIO Skills

- What CIOs Need To Know About Working With Partners: Techniques For CIOs To Use In Order To Be Able To Successfully Work With Partners

- Critical CIO Management Skills: Decision Making Skills That Every CIO Needs To Have In Order To Be Able To Make The Right Choices

- How CIOs Can Make Innovation Happen: Tips And Techniques For CIOs To Use In Order To Make Innovation Happen In Their IT Department

- CIO Communication Skills Secrets: Tips And Techniques For CIOs To Use In Order To Become Better Communicators

- Managing Your CIO Career: Steps That CIOs Have To Take In Order To Have A Long And Successful Career

- CIO Business Skills: How CIOs can work effectively with the rest of the company!

IT Manager Skills

- How IT Managers Can Make Innovation Happen: Tips And Techniques For IT Managers To Use In Order To Make Innovation Happen In Their Teams

- Staffing Skills IT Managers Must Have: Tips And Techniques That IT Managers Can Use In Order To Correctly Staff Their Teams

- Secrets Of Effective Leadership For IT Managers: Tips And Techniques That IT Managers Can Use In Order To Develop Leadership Skills

- IT Manager Career Secrets: Tips And Techniques That IT Managers Can Use In Order To Have A Successful Career

- IT Manager Budgeting Skills: How IT Managers Can Request, Manage, Use, And Track Their Funding

Negotiating

- Learn The Skill Of Exploring In A Negotiation: How To Develop The Skill Of Exploring What Is Possible In A Negotiation In Order To Reach The Best Possible Deal

- Learn How To Argue In Your Next Negotiation: How To Develop The Skill Of Effective Arguing In A Negotiation In Order To Get The Best Possible Outcome

- How To Open Your Next Negotiation: How To Start A Negotiation In Order To Get The Best Possible Outcome

- Preparing For Your Next Negotiation: What You Need To Do BEFORE A Negotiation Starts In Order To Get The Best Possible Deal

Miscellaneous

- Power Distribution Unit (PDU) Secrets: What Everyone Who Works In A Data Center Needs To Know!

- Making The Jump: How To Land Your Dream Job When You Get Out Of College!

How To Develop The Skill Of Effective Signaling In A Negotiation In Order To Get The Best Possible Outcome

This book has been written with one goal in mind – to show you how to successfully signal in your next negotiation. It's not easy being a negotiator and so we're going to show you how to successfully communicate to the other side what you really want them to do.

Let's Make Your Negotiation A Success!

What You'll Find Inside:

- **ESCALATION POWER: HOW TO USE IT, HOW TO DEFEND AGAINST IT**

- **THE SECRET TO DEALING WITH DEADLINES: WHAT NEGOTIATORS NEED TO KNOW**

- **SALES NEGOTIATORS NEED TO KNOW HOW TO WAIT**

- **5 TIPS FOR MAKING PEOPLE SEE THINGS YOUR WAY**

Dr. Jim Anderson brings his 25 years of real-world experience to this book. He's been a negotiator at some of the world's largest firms. He's going to show you what you need to do (and not do!) in order to get the best deal out of your next negotiation!

www.ingramcontent.com/pod-product-compliance
Lightning Source LLC
Chambersburg PA
CBHW071805170526
45167CB00003B/1176